SMYTHE GAMBRELL
LIBRARY

WESTMINSTER SCHOOLS

PRESENTED BY

Topher McGibbon
1980

SEA MONSTERS
of Long Ago

by Millicent E. Selsam

pictures by John Hamberger

Four Winds Press   New York

For Jennifer, Howard, and Boothby

The author and artist wish to thank
Dr. Eugene S. Gaffney, of the American
Museum of Natural History, for checking the
manuscript and illustrations for this book.

LIBRARY OF CONGRESS CATALOGING IN PUBLICATION DATA
Selsam, Millicent Ellis.
   Sea monsters of long ago.
   1. Dinosauria—Juvenile literature.　I. Hamberger,
John.　II. Title.
QE862.D5S4　　　　568'.1　　　　78-5385
ISBN　0-590-07567-5

Published by Four Winds Press
A division of Scholastic Magazines, Inc., New York, N.Y.
Text Copyright © 1977 by Millicent E. Selsam
Illustrations copyright © 1977 by John Hamberger
All rights reserved
Printed in the United States of America
Library of Congress Catalog Card Number: 78-5385
1　2　3　4　5　82　81　80　79　78

Millions and millions of years ago,
at the time of the dinosaurs,
strange-looking animals lived in the sea.

Like the dinosaurs, these animals were reptiles.
Some of them were small.
Others were giant size.
Some looked like fish.
Some looked like huge lizards.
And some looked like turtles with very
long necks.

We know what they looked like because
their skeletons have been found in the rocks.
The first skeleton was found by a
12-year-old girl
more than 150 years ago.

One day she saw some bones in the rock
at the edge of a cliff.
Scientists found out
it was the skeleton of
an ICHTHYOSAUR (**Ik**-thee-o-sawr).
Its name means fish lizard.
It looked like a fish.
But it had the bones of a reptile.

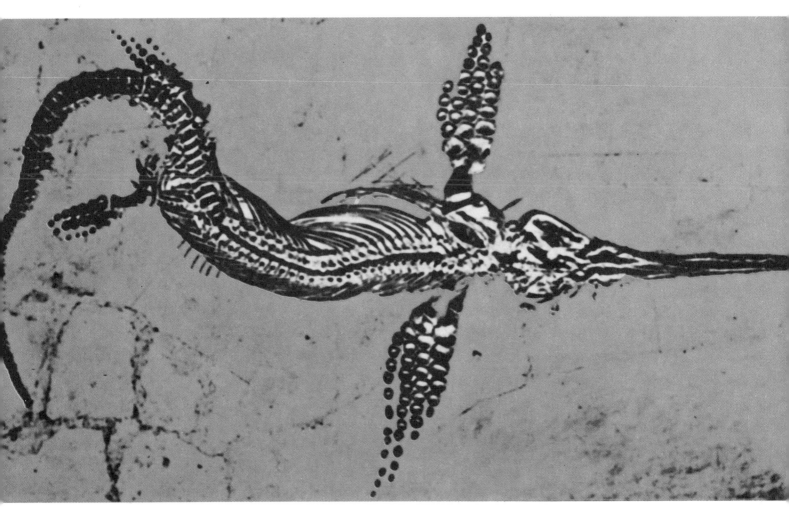

Ichthyosaur skeleton

Later, scientists found hundreds of other
Ichthyosaur skeletons.
Some of the skeletons had the skin preserved
around the bones.
You could tell exactly what this reptile
must have looked like 150 million years ago!

If you could see an Ichthyosaur today
you might think it was a dolphin or a shark.
Its long mouth was full of sharp teeth.
Its body was shaped like a fish.
It had a tail like a fish.

But it did not have gills like a fish.
It had lungs like all reptiles
so it had to come to the surface to get air.

From the bones we know that Ichthyosaurs
could swim very fast

Some Ichthyosaur skeletons had tooth marks on them.
The marks showed that they often fought
with each other.
Or they may have fought with other sea reptiles.

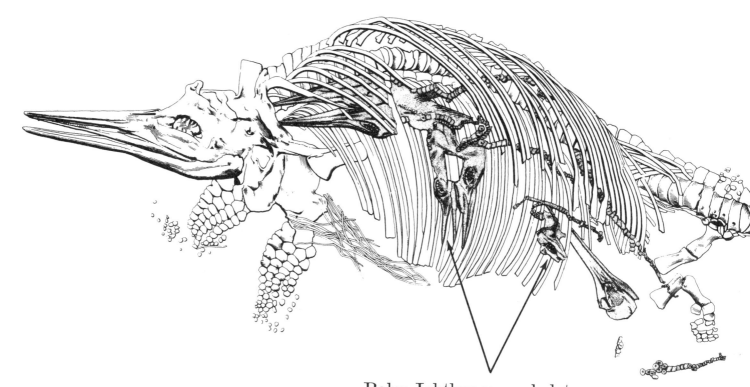

Baby Ichthyosaur skeletons

How did the Ichthyosaurs have their young?
Scientists knew that baby dinosaurs.
hatched from eggs laid on land.
But Ichthyosaurs lived in the sea and
reptile eggs cannot last long in sea water.
For a while it was a puzzle.
Then some new skeletons were found that
gave the answer.

The skeletons had baby skeletons inside them.
This showed that Ichthyosaurs kept their
eggs inside their bodies till they hatched.
Then the young were born alive right into
the sea!

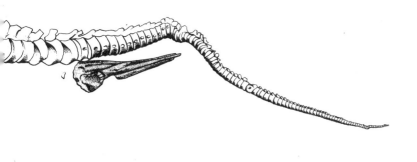

Not all Ichthyosaurs looked alike.
Many Ichthyosaurs were about ten feet long —
about the size of a car.
But one Ichthyosaur grew to 43 feet — about
the size of a city bus.
Its name was LEPTOPTERYGIUS (Lep-toe-ter-**idge**-i-us).

One Ichthyosaur had much bigger eyes than
the others.
Its eyes were as big as cereal bowls.
Its name was OPTHALMOSAURUS (Op-**thal**-mo-saw-rus).

One Ichthyosaur looked like a swordfish.
Its upper jaw was much longer than the
lower one.
Its name was EURINOSAURUS (Your-**rine**-o-saw-rus).

There were other strange reptiles in the sea
at the same time as the Ichthyosaurs.
They were called PLESIOSAURS (**Pleez**-ee-o-sawrs).
They had bodies like giant turtles
and small heads on very long necks.
They looked like the dragons of fairy tales.

This giant Plesiosaur was called
ELASMOSAURUS (Ee-**laz**-mo-saw-rus).

It was as long as four automobiles.
Its neck alone was two stories high.
It could reach out very far to grab fish.
Its mouth was full of sharp teeth.
It had four large flippers.
The flippers moved like oars.

Elasmosaurus had to breathe air.
Most likely it paddled along just below the
surface of the water.

Although most of the Plesiosaurs had long necks,
there were some with short necks
and long powerful skulls.
The biggest one of these was KRONOSAURUS (Kron-o-**saw**-rus).
It was about the size of an average whale.
Its head alone was ten feet long.
Its teeth were as sharp as knives.
Kronosaurus hunted the other sea reptiles.

There were still other kinds of giant
reptiles in the sea.
They were called MOSASAURS (**Mo**-sa-sawrs).
They looked like giant lizards.

One of them was called TYLOSAURUS (**Tile**-o-saw-rus).
It was thirty feet long — as big as
a great white shark!
It had a thick heavy body that flipped from
side to side as it swam through the water.
It really looked like a monster with its
huge head, huge jaws, and large mouth
filled with sharp teeth.

In the islands of the Pacific Ocean there is
a relative of the Mosasaurs.
It is called the Komodo dragon.
It is the largest living lizard in the
world today.
But it is only ten feet long — one third the
size of Tylosaurus.

What happened to Tylosaurus and all the other
strange reptiles that lived in the sea?
They swam in the oceans of the world
until about 70 million years ago.
Then they disappeared, just as the dinosaurs did.
Nobody knows why.

This chart shows when the Sea Monsters lived.

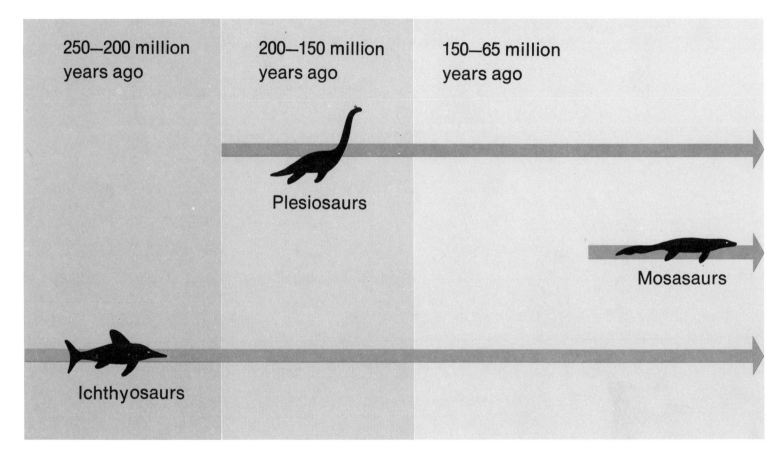

250—200 million years ago

200—150 million years ago

150—65 million years ago

Plesiosaurs

Mosasaurs

Ichthyosaurs